THE MAGNETIC NORTH

THE MAGNETIC NORTH

Mike Beedell
with a foreword by
Bill Mason

Toronto
Oxford University Press
1983

*This book is dedicated to my parents, my grandparents,
my brothers, and all my family*

ACKNOWLEDGEMENTS

Many thanks are due to the friends and companions
on so many trips who patiently waited while I took
'just one last shot' for the umpteenth time; to Wally
Schaber of *Trail Head*, who first sent me north; to
all the friendly northerners who gave me valuable
advice, good food, warm lodgings, and fascinating
stories which inspired me further on my
wanderings; and to Roger Boulton, who believed in
this project and helped me through to its
completion.

CANADIAN CATALOGUING IN PUBLICATION DATA
Beedell, Mike, 1956–
    The magnetic north

ISBN 0-19-540317-7

1. Canada, Northern — Description and travel —
Views.*   I. Title.

FC3956.B43   917.9'0022'2   C83-098702-9
F1060.5.B43

Produced by Roger Boulton
Designed by Fortunato Aglialoro

Printed and bound in Singapore by
FEP International Pte Ltd.

ISBN 0-19-540317-7

1234 – 6543

Foreword

I have always believed that the intensity of an artist's response to a scene or a place will depend in some measure on how he got there. The faster we travel, the less we see; the more facile our journey, the more forgettable it is. The explorer who hikes the uplands on foot, or slowly makes headway up-river by canoe, or laboriously works across a mountainside on skis, has more to tell than the casual sightseer who comes by plane, or helicopter, power-boat, or car. Perception is won by experience; we come to know our subjects by living with them, and we must work hard for the knowledge that we render into artistic forms.

The photograph that ends this book, of a mountaineer on the summit of Mt Logan, was taken by a man who had himself climbed all the way up there, even though he had never climbed a major mountain before. There, on the peak, is his companion, the rope that joins the two of them clearly visible in the picture, the mountain ranges of the Yukon spread out far below. This is a brave and classic image. The photographer's description of it is the more telling for its modesty and understatement. He could have written a book about this one experience alone; instead he prefers to let the pictures speak for themselves.

The sequence of polar bear shots is intimate and even charming. Only once, says Mike Beedell, has he met a bear that was vicious, terrorized him, wanted to 'make a meal' out of him. He does not tell us how nearly the bear succeeded. Mike had gone up into a watchtower miles from anywhere in the Churchill region, intending to photograph bears. Sure enough, they came around, but this one decided to have the man out of the tower. For three days and nights the bear attacked, rushing the stairs, bashing down the door, undeterred even by warning shots. A large rock, bounced off its head from a few feet above, only made the bear sit down, shake its head and lay off for a few hours' rest. Even after Mike had given it the slip, and was on his way to Churchill, the bear still gave pursuit.

In describing the rapids of the Little Nahanni River, Mike says that he and his partner 'sunk miserably right at the end'. To put that in perspective I should add that he is one of the best whitewater canoeists around. Here again, his descriptions are understatements, casual comments to exceptional photographs.

Mike Beedell is an exceptional fellow. Though he is young, he has in a few years gathered a wealth of wilderness experience, and has earned the loyalties of many people, for his skills as a guide, for the quality of his leadership, and for his high good humour on the trail. One story may stand for many. On a northern whitewater canoe trip his party camped for a special meal—I believe it was somebody's birthday. Mike excused himself and went off behind a bush, as it seemed for the most banal of reasons. He reappeared in the campfirelight dressed in a full tuxedo, with watch-chain and hat. He had somehow carried this outfit for hundreds of miles through the wilderness to wear it for this one occasion.

Although he is always good company, with such a keen sense of fun, he is never happier than when he is camping or canoeing alone for months on end. At one time during the making of this book his publisher got a letter from a Winnipeg hospital. 'Until yesterday,' it said, 'I was headed into the Barrens. Now I'm a thousand miles south and about to have my appendix out. . . . I guess I'm fortunate though, because I was going to go up the coast by freighter canoe with some Inuit hunters a few days ago. I would have been in the midst of appendicitis among the icebergs 400 miles from nowhere'. After that there was an ominous silence for nearly eighteen months, until a reassuring phone call from Cambridge Bay, where Mike had just been confined to his tent for a week by a blizzard, while photographing muskoxen. The call was collect, recalls the editor ruefully. As Mike says in his introduction, Arctic travel is expensive.

Of Auyuittuq National Park he once wrote enthusiastically, 'had 2000 square miles to myself. There wasn't another soul. . . . It was a really superb experience. I'd say this park offers the best ski-touring in the world but nobody knows about it. However, it's also the best place to crack your skull, break a leg, get crushed by a hurtling boulder or drown.'

Thanks to the medium of photography, the reader runs none of these risks. Instead an amazing range of colourful experience is set before us. Here then is the magnetic, magnificent North, ours to appreciate and enjoy.

BILL MASON, 1983

Introduction _____

'Thank God! there is always a Land of Beyond
For us who are true to the trail;
A vision to seek, a beckoning peak,
A farness that never will fail....'

Robert Service: 'The Land of Beyond'
Rhymes of a Rolling Stone, 1912

Ask any North American what first comes to mind at the mention of Canada and the answer will most likely relate in some way to 'the northern wilderness'. It is often said that the North has shaped our Canadian identity; it may be truer to say that our notions of the North have given rise to somewhat mythical notions of ourselves. Are we in fact a northern people? What is this 'northernness' that we like to claim for ourselves? We poeticize the cry of the loon, but how many of us have ever heard the clatter of caribou on the march or the bellow of a walrus? Few of us will ever in our lives have the chance to see the North, that 'Land of Beyond', yet the North has been a pervasive influence on our history and will probably play a major role in our future.

This vast expanse of the earth's surface—the Yukon, the Northwest Territories and Arctic Quebec—is more than just 'the last great frontier'. Beyond the sixtieth parallel is a land of well over one and a half million square miles or something like four million square kilometres in extent. The 'Great White North' is really half our country. Canada, being larger than China or the U.S.A., runs to extremes, and one of them is the North; it certainly stretches a long way. Going due north from Toronto we must travel farther to Pond Inlet on Baffin Island than we would in a southerly direction to Kingston, Jamaica, or to Mexico City. For all the talk of concern about the Mackenzie Valley pipeline and the oil-drilling in the Beaufort Sea, we still probably think less of Tuktoyaktuk than we do of Trinidad, and less of the Nahanni than we do of Nassau.

Distance is only one obstacle in travelling the Arctic; cost is another. A round trip to the North can cost several times as much as the same distance to any other quarter of the compass and when you get there the cost will have only just begun.

Then there is the environment to contend with—'nine months of winter and three months of bugs', as a disgruntled northerner once said. The North does not yield its beauty nor its satisfactions easily. Various native cultures show us how to live there in harmony with the wilderness, and one of the most astonishing examples of adaptation in the history of man is the culture of the Inuit, but we southerners can expect to come to terms with the North only very slowly and over a long period of several generations. Even today this immense land, one quarter of the entire continent, is home to only the same number of people as live in a medium-sized industrial town of the South.

For these and many other reasons we know little of the North, but ignorance here is not the same thing as indifference. The North has captured men's imaginations in every age. Canadians are northerners in their curiosity at least; we sense that not only the past but the future of North America will be very much bound up with that awesome world beyond the sixtieth parallel.

The 'magnetic North', a land of mystery, legend and grandeur; it beckons to romantics, adventurers, gold-diggers, painters, poets, explorers and solitaries alike. Whether in search of wisdom, wealth or fame, men have been drawn for centuries by an insatiable urge to see and experience this magical land.

Although I have travelled widely all over Canada and know many parts of the country very well, I find that no other place leaves me as spellbound as the North. Ever since I first saw the Central Barrens as a wilderness guide several years ago, I have travelled constantly in search of northern images. I have flown, driven, skied, hiked, paddled and climbed there. As soon as I come back south again, where I was born and grew up, I long to go north once more. In short, I have become an addict of the North and it is an obsession from which I have no wish to be cured.

The North abounds with startling contrasts— spectacular landscapes and desert wastes; a land where months of constant darkness give way at last to months of dazzling light, a land at one moment lifeless, at another teeming with a host of migrant animals, where tall groves of trees thin out to leave nothing but single dwarf birches lonely on the Barrens, where the majestic silence of the icebergs is answered by the roar of whitewater and the thunder of cataracts. These are some of the memories that have gone into this book, along with the recognition of a colourful past and an ancient culture caught in the press of change, threatened with upheaval by technologies acting on a scale so vast that no existing knowledge can predict the outcome.

My love of the North has enriched and strengthened my knowledge and love of Canada. So long as we have the North as our hinterland, our inspiration, and our future, we are a uniquely fortunate people. Yet this heritage is one we dare not take for granted. It is in the hope of sharing my enjoyment of the North and of inspiring concern for its future that I have put together these images in this book.

MIKE BEEDELL, 1983

1 Sculpted by ocean currents into the likeness of a great bird, or of the Winged Victory, this magnificent iceberg, seen here at Pond Inlet, will wander on the winds and currents until it gradually melts and returns to the sea.

2 *(left)* An inukshuk—'man of stone' or 'something standing in place of a man'—looking out to Frobisher Bay. In the past the Inuit used these man-shaped cairns for navigation and as aids to hunting. Of varying sizes and complexities, inukshuks were built on headlands as markers; they would also be set along hilltops, in ranks on either side of a valley down which caribou would be driven. Frightened of the man-shapes above, the animals would converge into a confined area where they were ambushed and killed by the huntsmen.

3 Auyuittuq National Park in July—a hiker leaps over a stream on the Turner Glacier. Mt Asgard and Mt Loki are seen in the background. Auyuittuq National Park encompasses 8,300 sq. miles/21,500 sq. kms on southern Baffin Island. The winds there can be extremely fierce as the glacial air funnels through the narrow valleys. Several years ago in Pangnirtung, the village closest to the park, a howling wind blew the nursing station clean away and overturned a number of other buildings.

4 At Pond Inlet, on the farthest coast of Baffin Island, a finely carved crucifix looks out across the windswept waters of Eclipse Sound. This cross marks the most northerly Roman Catholic mission in the world.

5 Light skips across the surface of rushing water. The unique quality of light in the North is very exciting for a photographer; the soft, low light lingers on for hours as the sun dips slowly to the horizon.

6–10 A polar bear may grow as long as 8 ft/2.4 m and reach a weight of 1500 lb/700 kg. With a single blow of its massive paw, it can break the back of a 450 lb/200 kg seal. On occasion the polar bear will stalk a man if driven by hunger but is otherwise rarely aggressive unless provoked. Although I have photographed some thirty different polar bears at close range, I have met only one that was intent on making a meal of me. He was blatantly vicious, a hardened fighter with many battle-scars, who terrorized me for several days.

7

8

9

11 Cape Dorset, on the Foxe Peninsula of Baffin Island, is internationally renowned for its superb printmaking and its outstanding carvers. The wealth of imagination, the luxuriance of colour, and the beauty of form, that have flourished at Cape Dorset through the last several decades have earned this settlement an honoured place in the world of the visual arts.

It was near Cape Dorset that the famous Hudson's Bay Company ship, the *Nascopie*, sank in 1947.

12 *(left)* Hikers near the junction of the Parade and Turner glaciers, heading towards the base of Mt Asgard.

13 Dwarfed by the immensity of Mt Asgard, hikers make their way around the crevasses that guard the base of this monolith in Auyuittuq Park. Asgard, rising up sheer at a height of 6,600 ft / 2,000 m, has lured climbers from around the world to attempt its almost vertical face.

14 *(left)* The arctic hare will often think itself still camouflaged when in fact all the snow has melted away. In the High Arctic flocks of hare are encountered and some sightings report as many as 500 in a group.

15a *(above)* A red fox in the uplands of the Ruby Range sits near his den. The sandy alpine and subalpine slopes provide excellent denning for foxes, wolves and bears.

15b *(right)* One of the most sought-after inhabitants of the North is the arctic ground squirrel or siksik. The grizzly bear and the golden eagle include him as a major part of their diet, while owls, wolves and foxes also hunt him regularly. In turn, the siksik can be bold to the point of impudence and has no hesitation at stealing your food or chewing holes through your pack when you are camped for the night.

16 The sun dips low on an arctic lake behind a lonely black spruce that precariously sustains itself on the edge of the treeline. With a diameter of only three inches/7.5 cms it may yet be well over 400 years old. A microscope would be neeeded to reveal the annual rings of growth.

17 *(right)* Mount Loki was named after the Norse god of mischief. Seen in the glow of the midnight sun, the mountain sticks up like a titanic shark's fin from a sea of ice in Auyuittuq National Park.

18 *(left)* The end of the South Pangnirtung Fiord and the entrance to Auyuittuq National Park.

19 A small group of muskoxen form their defensive position on the tundra of Arctic Quebec. These fascinating beasts are native to parts of northern Canada and Greenland. Their fur is said to make the finest wool in the world.

20 *(left)* The relics of a Thule culture homesite at Lee Point, Ellesmere Island. These people were the direct ancestors of the present-day Inuit. They were superb hunters. In their fragile kayaks and umiaks the Thules followed the migrations of the gigantic bowhead whale. The ribs and baleen of the whale were used to build their homes.

21 Burial in many parts of the north is very difficult because of thin soil, solid rock and permafrost. In many places it is impossible to dig a grave. Instead soil and rocks are piled upon the coffin.

22 The signature of Samuel Hearne (1745–92), cut in limestone at Schooner Cove, near Fort Prince of Wales (at the site of Churchill, Manitoba) on Hudson Bay. Two years later Hearne was sent overland to find and explore the Coppermine River. His first attempts failed but he reached the river on his journey of 1771–72, becoming the first man to get to the Arctic Ocean overland. Hearne was one of the greatest explorers to travel through the North. He walked over 5,000 mls/8,000 kms across the vast tundra, seeking a northwest passage to the Orient, and the rich mineral deposits of which the native peoples had spoken.

23 *(right)* Tuktoyaktuk, now the main base for oil exploration in the Beaufort Sea.

24 *(left)* An Inuk hunter takes aim at a harp seal in Harbour Fiord, Ellesmere Island. It is ironic that while the rifle is very efficient at killing it can defeat its own purpose—in the summer a sea mammal sinks down into the arctic waters almost immediately after being shot. The traditional Inuit harpoon was equipped with a thong attached to a float, thus ensuring that the speared animal was rarely lost to the sea.

25 The noble gyrfalcon, for many centuries prized by the world's aristocracy, is principally found today in the Canadian north. Poaching of these birds has become a serious problem, because they will fetch prices in excess of $20,000 apiece on the black market. I came upon this falcon just as he was settling down to eat a ptarmigan. We were equally fascinated by each other and spent several hours getting acquainted.

26 Dave Serkoak is a member of the Asiamiut (which means 'the inland group') and the vice-principal of the public school at Eskimo Point. During his leisure time he enjoys being out on the land to hunt and maintain his trap line.

27 *(right)* Butchering a narwhal at Sidlerosik, a whaling camp near Pond Inlet.

28 *(left)* An Inuit boy at Sidlerosik enjoys a fresh piece of narwhal muktuk. The skin of this sea mammal is rich in vitamin C, with a concentration equal to that of citrus fruits. Certain animal parts, eaten raw, can provide a good cross-section of vitamins and prevent such diseases as the scurvy that plagued early white explorers.

29 Josepee Flaherty cleans a narwhal tusk of pure ivory. It may fetch over a thousand dollars. Josepee is the son of the famous photographer and writer Robert Flaherty who explored the arctic regions of northern Quebec in the early 1900's.

30 Preparing fish for the freezers at the arctic char plant in Cambridge Bay. This plant is the largest commercial char fishery in the world. Many of the local residents find seasonal employment here. From Cambridge Bay, the fish are flown to southern markets and throughout North America they are prized as a gourmet's delight. The Inuit name for Cambridge Bay was Ikalukiutsiak, meaning 'the fair fishing place'.

31 Peepaloosee and Annie of Grise Fiord are both over seventy years old.
They live in the most northern community of the Americas. From their
doorstep on the beach they enjoy watching the giant icebergs go floating by.

32 *(left)* Laden with artillery an Inuit prepares for the hunt. Though gasoline will be costing him six dollars a gallon and the motorboat five thousand or more, he may yet search the entire day and get only one or two seals. If he is lucky he will be paid fifteen to twenty dollars for a skin and the meat will feed his family for a few days.

33 In Kangiqsujuaq, Arctic Quebec, Father Dion of the Mission Ste Anne practises on the organ. For years he travelled to his parishioners by dog team, spending from two days to a full week on the trail and living in igloos along the way. Today he can hop into a Twin-Otter and reach these same communities in a few hours.

34 Weavers at the Pangnirtung tapestry shop have won international acclaim for their unique work.

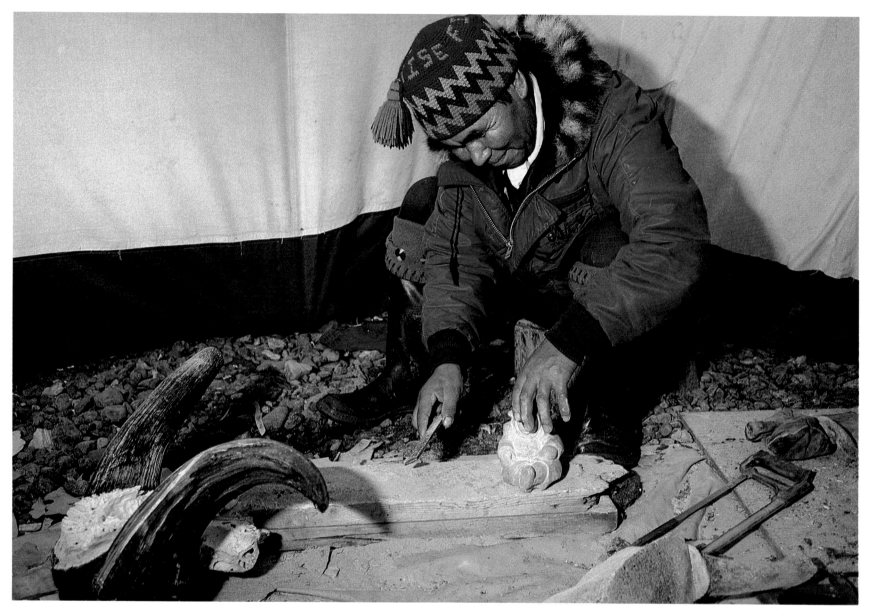

35 A native of Grise Fiord works in his carving tent on a soapstone sculpture. Muskoxen horns in the foreground may also be carved or used as embellishments on other works. Working in the tent may well be both more comfortable and less injurious to health than carving indoors, where poorly ventilated conditions, if they persisted, could lead to the contraction of such lung diseases as silicosis.

36 A young boy at Cambridge Bay enjoys the playground of this central arctic
community on Victoria Island.

37 The pride of the Dene people is seen in the handsome face of this young man; yet it is within the younger generation that the major cultural problems are most severe, many native youths being caught between two worlds and not knowing what direction they should take.

38 Myra Kaye of Old Crow loves to sit outside her home and smoke her pipe. She thinks she is somewhere between eighty and one hundred years old. She is a member of the Kutchin tribe and was born near Fort Yukon, Alaska.

39 Lucie Paluialok is said to be a shaman or 'wise woman', a person with the power to see the unseen, to mediate between the world of matter and the world of the spirits. The profession of shaman has characteristics of the witch doctor, as also of the religious mystic and the master of tribal ecstasy. In the past the shaman was credited with flights of the soul and used ecstatic trances to appease the gods, heal sickness and protect the clan. Today the practice of shamanism has almost disappeared under the influence of the Christian religion.

40 A mother and child view the Dene Games that are held every summer at Fort Rae. This town, 65 mls/104 kms from Yellowknife, is a stronghold of the Dene nation where most people are of the Slavey or Dog Rib tribe.

41 *(right)* Classic Inuit features of a young boy at Frobisher Bay.

42 A tranquil sea perfectly mirrors a gigantic iceberg at Fram Fiord, N.W.T. Most of the icebergs that travel through Canadian waters have calved off the glaciers of Greenland, only a short distance from Ellesmere Island.

43 *(right)* Inuit hunters in Jones Sound move along the coast at low tide. Small icebergs and pack ice are marooned near the shore until the water rises.

44 *(left)* The town of Pond Inlet, seen on a placid July day, with the mountains of Bylot Island in the background. Bylot is a bird sanctuary which is home during the summer months to the largest colony of snow geese in the world. The Pond Inlet region is extremely rich in bird life and in sea mammals. Ironically it lies just south of Lancaster Sound, through which the Arctic Pilot Project plans to run icebreaking supertankers carrying oil and gas from the arctic islands.

45 The komatiks, traditional Inuit sleds, are pulled up high above the tideline for the short summer season. In many arctic communities break-up does not come until late June or mid-July and freeze-up begins again in late September.

46 Kangiqsujuaq (Wakeham Bay) is a friendly, remote village in the hilly, rock-strewn region of Hudson Strait, Arctic Quebec. A glacial erratic is perched on the hill in the foreground.

47 *(right)* A small herd of walrus sits on an ice-pan near Lee Point, Ellesmere Island. These foul-smelling, belching, blubbery, great creatures can look hilarious as they roll about, but they can also be extremely dangerous. They will attack a boat if they think their young are threatened and a large walrus can even drown a polar bear.

48 *(left)* A Canadian Coast Guard ship, H.M.C.S. *Sir John Franklin*, travels through the very waters that the ill-fated Franklin expedition crossed in 1845–47. In this area history has lately been re-lived when arctic divers discovered the wreck of the *Breadalbane*. One of the ships that set out in search of the lost Franklin expedition, she sank off Beechey Island in 1853 and lies some 350 ft/ 100 m down, perfectly preserved by the frigid conditions.

49 Skiers ascend the Ogilvie Glacier, nearing the Yukon-Alaska border in Kluane.

50 Rich midnight colours set Hudson Bay aglow at the McConnell Bird
Sanctuary, near the border between the Northwest Territories and Manitoba.

51 A snowmobile moves across an expanse of ice in Ungava Bay near Kuuj-
juaq. In the distance, fragments of the treeline can be seen huddled in the folds
of the hills.

52 Soapstone carvings take shape at Allen Island, a polar bear hunting camp near Robinson Sound. The traditional Inuit sled or komatik makes a handy bench on which to sit and carve in the spring sun.

53 *(right)* Greg MacDonald and his family head out onto a bay near Yellowknife with their team of sled dogs. Eskimo dogs were at one point allowed to decline in numbers dangerously close to the point of extinction, all because of the popularity of the snowmobile. However, there has been a revival of interest in dogsled travel among both the natives and the whites, and the breed of dog has been stabilized.

54 *(left)* Oil burns off at a discovery well in the Beaufort Sea.

55 A large artificial island, built in the Beaufort Sea by Esso, as a way of drilling for oil 17 mls/30 kms off the mainland coast. The impact of such activity on these fragile surroundings is still not known. The technology needed to protect this environment from a full scale blow-out is still inadequate.

56 At the Anglican church in Pangnirtung a tiny Inuit girl, clad in her kamiks and Sunday best, clutches a native prayer book and eyes the camera uncertainly. The first arctic Anglican mission was established near here in 1884 at a whaling station on Blacklead Island in Cumberland Sound.

57 One of the most beautiful churches in the North is the Anglican church in
Frobisher Bay, adorned with a wealth of native artistry, a narwhal cross and
sealskin tapestries. Note the altar rail made of sleds or komatiks turned on
their sides.

58 Women at St Michael's Church in Fort Rae still observe the old practice of segregation from the men during a Sunday service.

59 This young Inuk is well clothed for the cold, with his thick ruff of wolf fur protecting his face from the wind. However, because of southern influence, many children no longer dress adequately for the climate. It is not uncommon to see a child walking to school in a baseball cap and a flimsy coat when the temperature is –30°F/ –34°C.

60 *(left)* The remnants of a white trader's boat which once plied the waters of the Porcupine and Yukon Rivers in search of furs. This region near Old Crow is one of the richest muskrat habitats in the world.

61 Today the common practice amongst the Inuit is to bury their dead; however in the past some groups wrapped their dead in caribou robes and left them on the tundra. This particular coffin belonged to a dead shaman. This shaman was not buried because it was believed that burying shamans hindered their ability to go on soul flights, which could take them as far as the moon.

62 *(left)* The mine at Nanisivik is one of the safest of hard rock mines, due to the permafrost here which penetrates the earth as deep as 1000 ft/300 m. The warmer summer air coming into the tunnels creates a myriad of ice crystals and accounts for the delicate glitter of light.

63 The multi-coloured igloo-shaped homes of Nanisivik are an attractive aspect of this modern mining town near Admiralty Inlet—the largest fiord in the world. It was less than a decade ago that the establishment of a town here was made viable by the rich local deposits of zinc and lead.

64 Mists rise off the Coppermine River as it makes its journey through the September Mountains on its way to Coronation Gulf. Here the treeline clings to the river's edge, creating a microclimate and a haven for vegetation. Visible in the background are the true barrens, encompassing tens of thousands of square kilometres where upstanding trees can rarely exist.

65 A storm gathers strength on the lowlands of Hudson Bay. Here the treeline can be seen in the distance. Hardy spruce, bent and gnarled by the winds, stand at the beginning of the tundra.

66 This ore ship, docked at the Polaris Project, fills its hold with rich lead-zinc ore. Polaris is the most northern metal mine in the world, situated on Little Cornwallis Island near the north magnetic pole.

67 The 'Sky Coach' belongs to veteran northern pilot Willie Laeserich, who has saved many lives by 'med-evacs', the airlifting of people who are in medical emergencies. His planes have become flying nurseries on several occasions when mothers have given birth *en route*. My first flight with him took a doctor and myself on what I thought was to be a sightseeing tour but, within twenty minutes of being in the air, we got an alert from Pelly Bay where a mother was in labour. The doctor told me to stand by as 'midwife' on our flight to the Yellowknife hospital, but turbulence was so bad that I was soon in a worse state than the mother.

68 Larch trees, the only evergreens to shed their foliage in winter, stand bravely at the edge of the treeline in Ungava Bay.

69 *(right)* A piper plays to the children of Pangnirtung on a cool spring evening. He is newly come from Scotland, hired by the Hudson's Bay Company to man one of their many posts in the North.

70 *(left)* Iceberg, Grise Fiord, NWT.

71 A northerner heads out onto the pack-ice of Hudson Bay in search of seals. He will travel to the flow edge where sea-mammals congregate and move with the flux of ice.

72 The Watson Lake signposts are an extraordinary array of international road signs and memorabilia which have been stolen or 'borrowed' from the byways of the world. People travelling on the Alaska Highway add to this collection every year.

73 An old, weathered, equipment cache, roofed and patched with flour tins,
keeps valuable equipment safe from rodents and other vermin.

74 *(left)* Yukon River at Dawson City, Yukon.

75 Whitehorse, the capital of the Yukon, gained its importance through being the terminus of the Whitepass Railway and having a major airfield during the building of the Alaska Highway. The town was named after a series of rapids called 'the white horses' which were stilled by a dam up-river. Today White-horse is a city of contrasts, with quaint log cabins sandwiched between modern office blocks.

76 *(left)* A young Inuit mother and child near Cambridge Bay watch as their father goes out fishing on an inland lake on Victoria Island.

77 George Gilbert, Inspector of Mines for the Yukon, examines gold dust at a small placer gold camp along the Yukon River. Many small operators make a handsome profit from a summer's work and some do not find it necessary to work for the rest of the year.

78 An August moon rises over White Sandy Lake, an enchanting area of rolling hills and eskers east of Great Bear Lake.

79 *(right)* Midnight at Yellowknife, looking onto Great Slave Lake. Great Slave is over 2000 ft/ 600 m deep and supports a commercial fishery netting large stocks of lake trout and whitefish.

80 *(left)* The North Canol Road was built during World War II by the Americans to rush a pipeline from Norman Wells to Whitehorse. In 1945, soon after its completion, they decided to abandon the project. Vehicles were parked neatly at the side of the road and left. For years many of these vehicles provided transportation and spare parts for the inhabitants of the region. A few vintage machines—minus wheels and motors—can still be found standing where they were parked thirty-eight years ago. The cost of the pipeline and the road was in the neighbourhood of 130 million dollars. Today this road provides access into the interior of the Yukon and the Mackenzie Mountains.

81 Neskataheen is an historic native village on the part of the gold rush route called the Dalton Trail. All that now remains of the village is the graves and the spirit houses. The latter were built above the graves of the Stick Indians to shelter and comfort the spirits of the dead.

82 Arctic cotton-grass on an alpine slope in the Yukon.

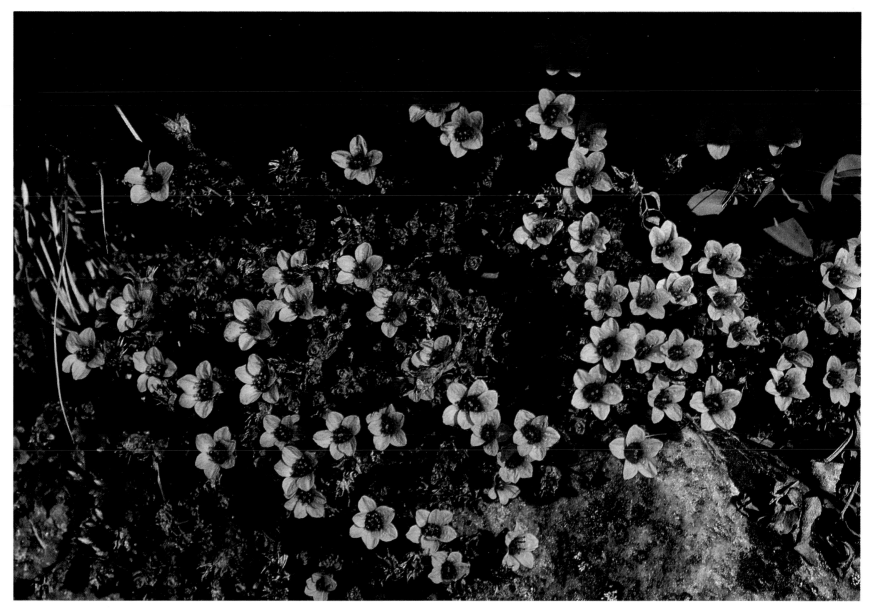

83 Purple saxifrage, a hardy alpine and arctic flower, finds its niche among
the jumbled boulders and rock-strewn wastelands of the North.

84 The end of the Kaskawulsh Glacier brings down immense piles of medial and terminal morraine. The glacier forms the major source of the Slims River.

85 *(right)* Caribou, Ungava Bay, Quebec.

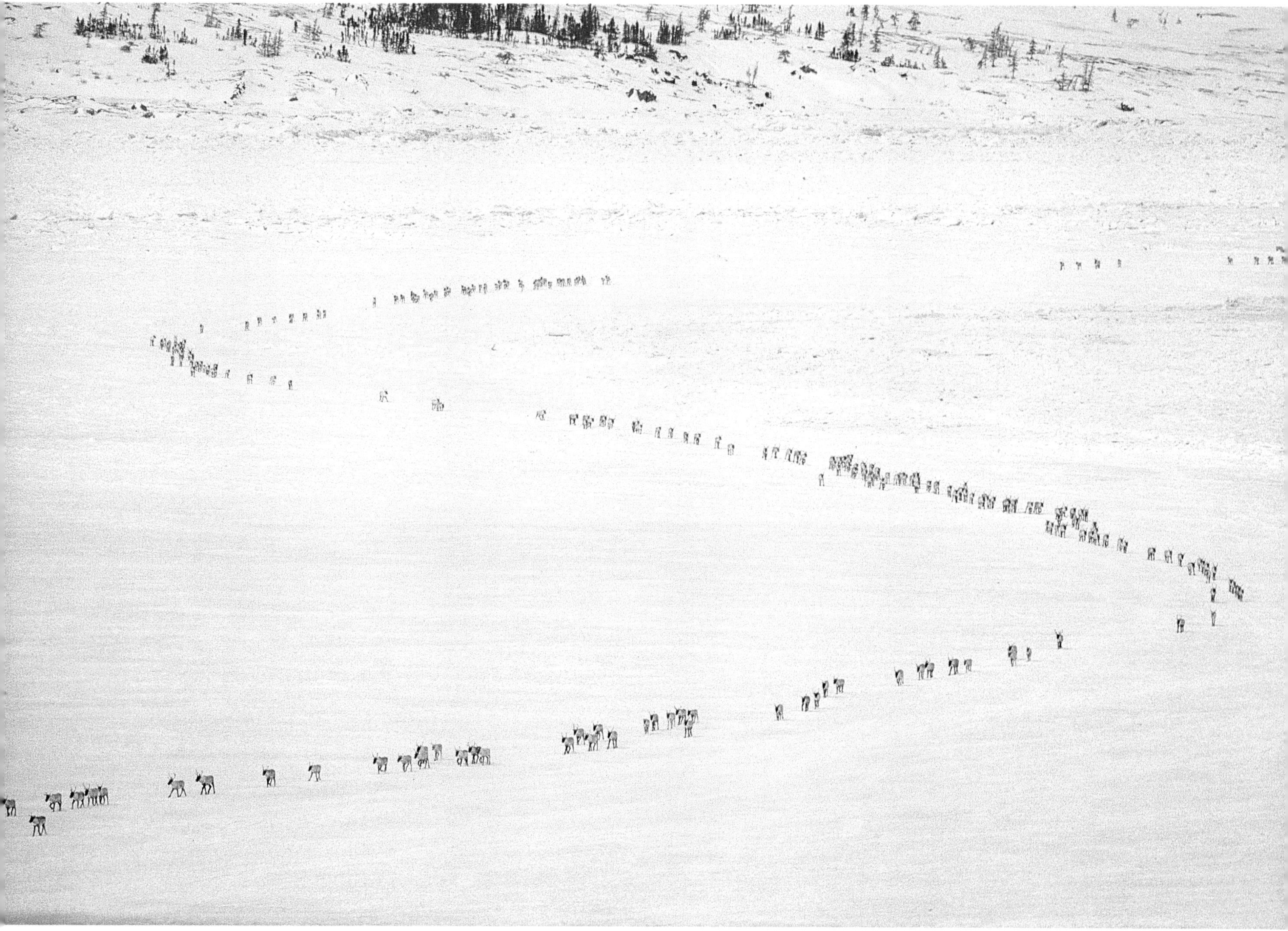

86-87 The George River caribou herd begins its eastern migration towards the Labrador calving grounds. This is the largest herd in North America and perhaps in the world, its numbers currently being estimated at close to 400,000 animals. I camped for a week near a major caribou crossing and watched in amazement as thousands and thousands of animals clattered by me day and night. From my hilltop I could see a continuous string of caribou nearly two kilometres long.

88 *(left)* Mount Maxwell is the first to catch the early morning sun at the point where the Kaskawulsh Glacier pushes its snout into the Slims River Valley. This region has the highest concentration of grizzly bears in North America.

89 A caribou antler lies at the edge of Red Rock Lake in the Central Barrens. Antlers are dropped annually and they can be found scattered along the migration routes and feeding areas of the caribou. They are an important source of calcium for a variety of rodents.

90 There are approximately 50,000 sq. mls/ 130,000 sq. kms of fresh water in the Northwest Territories. One is made aware of this when flying over the Central Barrens from Bathurst Inlet to Yellowknife. In all directions stretches an enchanting expanse of lakes and rivers.

91 *(right)* Sunset on Point Lake, one of the vast Arctic lakes whose enormous volume gives force to the waters of the Coppermine River as it rushes on its way to the Arctic Ocean.

92 *(left)* An evening at Water Pass, looking at an unnamed peak in the St Elias Range.

93 A view from the flank of Mt Logan at 15,000 ft/4,500 m and looking west into Alaska.

94 Evening light sets the hills aglow near Kluk-shu on the Haines Road. Near here natives still catch huge salmon in traditional fishing weirs as the fish fight their way up a tributary of the Tatshenshini River.

95 *(right)* Midnight in June; our camp at 18,000 ft/5,500 m on the Logan Plateau, Kluane National Park. In the background the West Summit is still aglow with the light of an untiring sun.

96 *(left)* The Selwyn mountains on the South Nahanni River.

97 A solitary hiker walks along a snowfield on Amphitheatre Mountain in the Burwash Uplands, an area abundant with dall sheep and Osborne cari-bou. I met my first grizzly bear on the flanks of this mountain while I was hiking alone. My lens drew me to him, while my instincts pulled me back. The result was an uncontrollable shake and no picture to record the encounter.

98 Hiking in early June beneath Mt Hoge , near Badlands Creek, Yukon.

99 *(right)* In the Kluane icefields a skier ventures towards a series of blow-outs on the Seward Glacier. These gigantic holes are believed to be caused by the carving action of glacial winds. The icefields of Kluane comprise some 7,500 sq mls/ 20,000 sq. kms of a total area of 8,500 sq mls/ 22,000 sq. kms. For a period of three weeks our little group of skiers had this entire region to itself. In May and June the region offers some of the best ski-touring and telemarking in the world.

100 A pingo sticks out of the flat expanse of the delta near Tuktoyaktuk. These hills are created by the upswelling of solid ice cores within the permafrost. At one time Tuktoyaktuk had a curling rink and a large community freezer which the locals had fashioned from the heart of a pingo.

101 *(right)* A view of the Duke River Valley and the Badlands Creek region from a lofty alpine ridge in the Burwash Uplands. This particular spot is a favourite perch for raptors, which is evident from the rich orange lichen growth visible on the rocks.

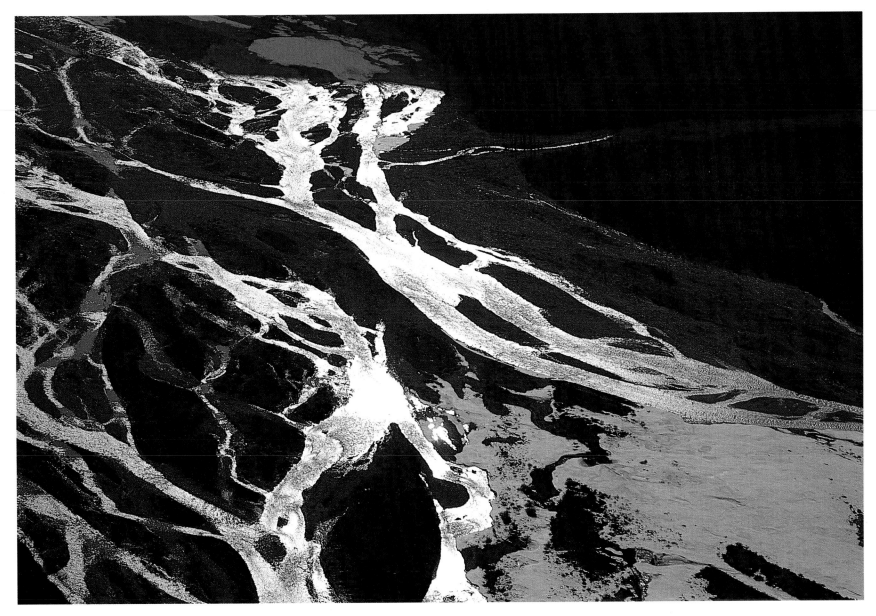

102 *(left)* Whitewater enthusiasts challenge the rapids of the Little Nahanni River. This is an extremely turbulent watercourse of dangerous canyons and boulder-strewn rapids feeding the South Nahanni. After successfully dodging the boulders for miles, my partner and I have nevertheless sunk miserably right at the end of the rapids.

103 A braided tributary of the Carcajou River rushes from the Mackenzie Mountains during spring runoff.

104 *(left)* Hikers venture between the sheer walls of Prairie Creek in Nahanni National Park.

105 Virginia Falls in Nahanni National Park is an outstanding spectacle of nature's power. The waters drop 316 ft/100 m, twice the height of Niagara, and there are approximately 4 acres/1.6 hectares of water on the face. I have sat for hours near the brink, mesmerized by the raw energy and power of this cataract. Thanks to the Parks system this marvel is safe from developers and dams (see also plates 107–9).

106 The Mackenzie Mountains extend for some 500 mls/800 kms from the South Nahanni Valley to the Bonnet Plume River. They are a hiker's paradise, with high alpine ridges and a variety of big animals. This is accordingly a popular region for trophy hunters.

107 *(right)* I know of nothing more spiritually exhilarating than to travel alone through beautiful wilderness landscapes. On a solo journey down the Nahanni I took this photograph of myself at the 'Sluice Box' just above the point where the river hurls itself over the Virginia Falls.

108 The Brink, Virginia Falls, South Nahanni River.

109 *(right)* The Base, Virginia Falls, South Nahanni River.

110 *(left)* A rainbow evolves as sunshowers move across the mountains near Desdeash Lake. This region is accessible by the Haines Road which leads to the coastal town of Haines in Alaska.

111 Sunshowers at some limestone ramparts, which mark the northeastern boundary of Kluane National Park. The cliffs are a favourite nesting place for golden eagles. These noble birds can often be seen soaring on the thermal currents above this alpine region.

112 Gold nuggets from the Klondike goldfields, Yukon.

113 An oxbow formation on the Yukon River above Dawson.

114a–114b Diamond Tooth Gertie's in Dawson, the only legal casino in the country, usually plays to a full house all summer long. Here you can gamble and drink into the small hours of the morning, while the dance girls strut the stage. Diamond Tooth Gertie herself was a famous dancehall girl of goldrush days. Her fellow entertainers, such as Snake Hips Lulu and Glass-Eyed Annie, were famous for their way of making money from the wide-eyed men of the Klondike. A unique mixture of rugged and refined characters can be found at Gertie's on any one night.

115 *'Where are the dames I used to know*
In Dawson in the days of yore?...
Gay dance-hall girls of Dawson Town.'
Robert Service

116 At the tree-line, south of Eskimo Point.

117 *(right)* Midnight on Coronation Gulf as the sun travels along the horizon and begins its morning ascent. I paddled out onto this amazing scene after a month-long canoe journey on a nearby river. The air was so cold that the water froze to my paddle and I simply drifted on while contemplating this beautiful sight.

118 *(left)* Sailboats on Back Bay in Yellowknife almost suggest a Caribbean scene; but sailboat enthusiasts here must enjoy the rather more frigid waters of Great Slave Lake, 11,200 sq. mls/ 30,000 sq. kms of them.

119 Aurora borealis, Ungava Bay, Arctic Quebec.

120 *(left)* Cresting a hill in the Badlands Creek region, Burwash Uplands, Yukon.

121 Igloo on a ski expedition, Ungava Bay, Arctic Quebec.

122 The Whitepass Railway was begun in 1898, running from Skagway in Alaska to Whitehorse. It superseded the tortuous Chilkoot Pass trekking route which had taken the lives of so many men and killed thousands of horses. The 110 ml/176 km track has incredibly steep elevations to contend with as it climbs from sea level at Skagway to the B.C. border and then into the Yukon near Carcross.

123 *(right)* A team of sled dogs on the Keewatin coast. They will spend an entire winter without shelter from the howling winds.

124 A full northern moon rises over the Yukon River just above the city of Whitehorse. In the past, scores of huge stern-wheelers steamed the waters from the Bering Sea to Carcross, delivering goods and passengers for the interior of the Yukon.

125 *(right)* A classic Yukon sunrise silhouettes a stand of spruce along the Dempster Highway and the North Klondike River.

126 Clinging to the summit ridge of Mount Logan on a windy June evening, a climber reaches the top at 19,525 ft/ 5,951 m. Situated deep in the icefields of Kluane National Park, Logan is the highest peak in Canada and the second highest in North America. It was first climbed in 1925. Photographing an ascent in 1979 was the most difficult thing that I have ever done in my life. Too often my exhaustion was such that I could not even lift my camera. Altitude sickness, hallucinations and daily nausea set me wondering what it was all about, but the landscape was so amazing as to make it worthwhile. All the same, from now on I'll be quite content to look for spiritual fulfilment at somewhat lesser altitudes.